My First Acrostic

Southern Scotland Inspirations

Edited by Donna Samworth

First published in Great Britain in 2009 by:

Young Writers
Remus House
Coltsfoot Drive
Peterborough
PE2 9JX
Telephone: 01733 890066
Website: www.youngwriters.co.uk

All Rights Reserved
© Copyright Contributors 2009
SB ISBN 978-1-84924-421-3

Foreword

The 'My First Acrostic' collection was developed by Young Writers specifically for Key Stage 1 children. The poetic form is simple, fun and gives the young poet a guideline to shape their ideas, yet at the same time leaves room for their imagination and creativity to begin to blossom.

Due to the young age of the entrants we have enjoyed rewarding their effort by including as many of the poems as possible. Our hope is that seeing their work in print will encourage the children to grow and develop their writing skills to become our poets of tomorrow.

Young Writers has been publishing children's poetry for over 19 years. Our aim is to nurture creativity in our children and young adults, to give them an interest in poetry and an outlet to express themselves. This latest collection will act as a milestone for the young poets and one that will be enjoyable to revisit again and again.

Contents

Addiewell Primary School, West Calder
Kyle Hamilton (6) 1
Ty McAulley (6) 2
Iain Brown (6) 3
Amie Long (7) 4
Zoe Carruthers (7) 5
Paul Duncan (6) 6
Adam McGillivray (7) 7
Josh Carruthers (6) 8
Cameron Kane (6) 9

Cairn Primary School, Maybole
Katie Harper (7) 10
Thomas Currie (7) 11
Eilidh Mackay (7) 12
Eilidh Summers (7) 13
Euan Campbell (8) 14
Ebony MacPherson (8) 15
Ruth Dowie (7) 16
Sarah McElroy (7) 17
Steffi Purdie (6) 18
Emily Maxwell (7) 19
Logan McClounie (7) 20
Sophie Hearton (7) 21
Chloe Gladstone (7) 22
Douglas Strachan (6) 23
Calum Murray (6) 24
Jade Hepburn (8) 25
Brooke Watson (6) 26
Tia McLanaghan (6) 27
Harry McKenna (6) 28

Carnbroe Primary School, Coatbridge
Jade Arthur (7) 29
Jessica Dunion (6) 30
Freya Crawley (6) 31
Rachael Mackay (6) 32
Justin Harvie (7) 33
Craig Renicks (6) 34
Craig Kerr (7) 35
Lewis McKean (6) 36

Jonathan Grabiec (6) 37
Hannah Dunion (6) 38
Meer Faysal Ahmed (6) 39

Coaltown of Wemyss Primary School, Kirkcaldy
Cameron Bell (6) 40
Denni Brown (8) 41
Emily Rose Dick (6) 42
Adam Dixon (5) 43
Ben Dryburgh (6) 44
Ellie Fraser (5) 45
Marina Hendren (6) 46
Connor MacCuish (7) 47
Kye Pickard (5) 48
Erin Rhodes (7) 49
Luke Rolland (5) 50
Molly Walker (5) 51
Rosie Walker (7) 52

Dairsie Primary School, Cupar
Adam Bruce Hart (7) 53
Kerri Stalker (7) 54
Louise Moncrieff (6) 55
Lewis Moyes (7) 56
David Reay (6) 57
Chrissy Newton-Sutherland (6) 58

Dalgety Bay Primary School, Dalgety Bay
Conall Moyes Wallace (7) 59
Hannah Eadie (6) 60
Abbey Kerr (6) 61
Jamie Dawson (7) 62
William McPhee White (7) 63
Tiffanie McColl (7) 64
Bethany Leitch (6) 65
Rachel Rowntree (7) 66
Sean Bartholomew (6) 67
Ryan Daley (6) 68
Ryan Harrison (6) 69
Ryan Aitken (6) 70
John Ardila-Neville (6) 71
Saci Marton (6) 72

Max Johnston (7) ... 73
Leah Murray (6) ... 74
Andrew Elliott (6) ... 75
Ross Williamson (7) ... 76
James Uphill (6) ... 77
Abby Paveling (6) ... 78
Emma Stuart (6) ... 79
Ewan Logan (6) ... 80
Chloe Megen Dominy (6) ... 81

Dalry Primary School, Dalry
Naomi Calley (6) ... 82
Travis Blakely (6) ... 83
Andrew Allan (7) ... 84
Luke Stalker (6) ... 85
Cameron Shaw (6) ... 86
Isabelle Hill (6) ... 87
Adam Gilbert (7) ... 88
Marni Caig (7) ... 89
Amy Murphy (6) ... 90
Abigail Campbell (6) ... 91
Dale Martin (6) ... 92
Jade McCafferty (6) ... 93
Eilidh Stewart (6) ... 94
Jenna Russell (6) ... 95
Brooke Neill (7) ... 96

Houston Primary School, Houston
Jennifer Boyd (5) ... 97
Isaac Nayar (6) ... 98
Innes Durrant (6) ... 99
Lewis McGeachin (6) ... 100
Catherine Abdallah (5) ... 101
Amy Lawson (5) ... 102
Abby Birrell (5) ... 103
Leah Feely (5) ... 104
Robyn Stirling (5) ... 105
Daniel Hatfield (5) ... 106
Hannah Robertson (5) ... 107
Katy Mitchell (5) ... 108
Harris Cunningham (5) ... 109
Louis Jeffrey (5) ... 110

Macmerry Primary School, Macmerry
Bethany Catchpole (6) ... 111
Niamh Renwick (6) ... 112
Zara Johnston (6) ... 113

Markinch Primary School, Markinch
Ruby Stewart (8) ... 114
Aislinn Wilkie (7) ... 115
Rebeka Korosi (8) ... 116
Liana Fergus (8) ... 117
Nadia Ali (8) ... 118
Morgan Birrell (8) ... 119
Andrew Milne (8) ... 120
Kayley McKenzie (8) ... 121
Ryan Wilson (7) ... 122
Charlotte Mackenzie (8) ... 123
Kyle Anderson (8) ... 124
Liam Gregory (8) ... 125
Aidan Duff (8) ... 126
Matthew Barrie (8) ... 127
Ryan Todd (7) ... 128

St Bernard's Primary School, Coatbridge
Jay Rowley (7) ... 129
Necole Lannigan (7) ... 130
Jordan McCann (7) ... 131
Kieran McGrath (8) ... 132
Aidan Duffy (7) ... 133
Rocco Rossetti (7) ... 134
Bethany Martin (7) ... 135
Lily McGuire (7) ... 136
Andrew Cullen (8) ... 137
Liam Hamilton (7) ... 138

St Marie's Primary School, Kirkcaldy
Angel McIlhatton (7) ... 139
Josh Leblanc (7) ... 140
Bethany Kinnaird (7) ... 141
Calum Robertson (7) ... 142
Megan Rae (7) ... 143
Rhys Maksymuik (7) ... 144
Ricky Keatings (7) ... 145
Andrew Doherty (7) ... 146
Rachel McGregor (7) ... 147
Olivia Taylor (7) ... 148
Kara Gallacher (7) ... 149
Sophie Hockham (7) ... 150
Kirstin Anderson (7) ... 151
Joseph Ciaraldi (7) ... 152

St Mary's Primary School, Largs

Michael Kelly, Andrew Burns (6) &
Luca Faccenda (7) 153
Amy Mullen & Hannah Muir (6) 154
Megan Pratt & Megan Ward (6) 155
Daniel McGowan &
Lauren McCaig (6) 156
Megan Kelly (6) &
Christopher McKinlay (7) 157
Brooke Perry & Kian Murdoch (6) 158
Stan Rodger & Anna Capocchi (6) 159

St Mary's Primary School, Lanark

Alyx Mackie (7) 160
Chloe Marshall (7) 161
Tové McCarthy (7) 162
Kerry Noble (6) 163
Mark Scott (6) 164
Erin Snow (7) 165
Mark Bustard (6) 166
Jordan Oakes (6) 167
Lewis Dowie (7) 168
Tanya Brennan (6) 169
Sam McFadyen (7) 170
John Gair (7) 171
Benji MacDonald (7) 172
Rachel Donnachie (6) 173
Enya McKnight (6) 174
Holly Smith (6) 175
Cameron Dickie (5) 176
Olivia Ferguson (5) 177
Keva Culkin (5) 178
Leoni Kay Fletcher (6) 179
Daniel Balmer (5) 180

Sheuchan Primary School, Stranraer

Shannon McCutcheon (7) 181
Niall Slavin (7) 182
Brook Chandler (7) 183
Joel Thomson (8) 184
Dawn Wyllie (7) 185
Emma Smith (8) 186
Robbie Wilson (8) 187
Gordon Forbes &
Lewis McCamon (7) 188
Callum Lees (7) 189

Towerbank Primary School, Edinburgh

Grace Peacock (6) 190
Hugo Boland (7) 191
Alexander Marriott (6) 192
Eva Donnelly (6) 193
Hamish Martin (7) 194
Jorgey Scott-Learmonth (6) 195

Whitecrook Primary School, Clydebank

Gavin Neil (7) 196
Cameron Henderson (6) 197
Josh Innes (6) 198
Sophie Anderson (6) 199
Jay Scott (6) 200
Liam Gallagher (6) 201
Zoe Young (7) 202

The Poems

My First Acrostic - Southern Scotland Inspirations

Spring

S unny days
P rimrose days
R ainbow days
I n the garden
N ew flowers
G reen buds.

Kyle Hamilton (6)
Addiewell Primary School, West Calder

Spring

S pring sun
P urple pansies
R ainbows
I see new lambs
N ew grass will come
G reen grass.

Ty McAulley (6)
Addiewell Primary School, West Calder

My First Acrostic - Southern Scotland Inspirations

Spring

S un
P urple pansies
R ain will come
I see the lambs
N ew baby birds
G reen grass.

Iain Brown (6)
Addiewell Primary School, West Calder

Spring

S pringtime is beautiful
P ink flowers growing in the fields
R ainbows go over the fields
I am holding a ladybird
N ew flowers
G reen leaves on the trees.

Amie Long (7)
Addiewell Primary School, West Calder

My First Acrostic - Southern Scotland Inspirations

Spring

S pringtime is beautiful
P ink flowers
R ainbows go over the fields
I am holding a butterfly
N ew baby lambs
G reen grass.

Zoe Carruthers (7)
Addiewell Primary School, West Calder

Spring

S un shines
P retty gardens
R ainbows sparkle
I ndigo
N ice weather
G reen grass.

Paul Duncan (6)
Addiewell Primary School, West Calder

My First Acrostic - Southern Scotland Inspirations

Spring

S unny days
P retty garden
R ainbow colours
I ndigo blossoms
N ew lambs
G reen grass.

Adam McGillivray (7)
Addiewell Primary School, West Calder

Spring

S unny
P retty
R ainbow
I see butterflies
N ew flowers
G reen grass.

Josh Carruthers (6)
Addiewell Primary School, West Calder

My First Acrostic - Southern Scotland Inspirations

Spring

S unny
P retty
R ainy
I ndigo
N ew flowers
G reen.

Cameron Kane (6)
Addiewell Primary School, West Calder

Me!

K atie is my name
A pples are my favourite food
T rusted with my Nintendo DS
I love Mrs Fyfe
E ilidh M and Eilidh S are my best friends.

Katie Harper (7)
Cairn Primary School, Maybole

My First Acrostic - Southern Scotland Inspirations

Thomas!

T homas, I'm nice and small
H appy chappie, that's me
O ften I play football with Steven
M &Ms and
A pples are my favourite
S teven is my good friend
That's me!

Thomas Currie (7)
Cairn Primary School, Maybole

Eilidh

E ilidh is my name
I have a sister Iona, I
L ove Mum, Dad and Iona
I love this school
D ivision is fun
H ealthy apples to eat.
   That's me!

Eilidh Mackay (7)
Cairn Primary School, Maybole

My First Acrostic - Southern Scotland Inspirations

Eilidh

E ilidh, that's me
I have a twin sister, I
L ove my mum and dad
I have a big brother
D odgeball is my favourite
H opping makes me sick!

Eilidh Summers (7)
Cairn Primary School, Maybole

Euan

E uan is my name
U sually I am playing rugby
A lways doing my best
N ever playing on my dad's Xbox, not me!

Euan Campbell (8)
Cairn Primary School, Maybole

My First Acrostic - Southern Scotland Inspirations

Ebony

E bony is my name, I have
B lue eyes and long hair
O n the 7th of April, it's my birthday
N ice girl, that's me! I am
Y oung and funny!

Ebony MacPherson (8)
Cairn Primary School, Maybole

Me!

R uth is my name
U sually I go out to play with Sarah
T rustworthy and responsible
H eather is my big sister and she cares for me.

Ruth Dowie (7)
Cairn Primary School, Maybole

My First Acrostic - Southern Scotland Inspirations

Me!

S arah is my name
A ble and trusted, that's me!
R uth is my best friend forever!
A lways helping my friends
H annah Montana is my favourite TV show.

Sarah McElroy (7)
Cairn Primary School, Maybole

Me!

S teffi is my name and
T ig is my game
E very day I play tig and my
F riends are Jade and Jack
F unny and friendly
I am the queen of language.

Steffi Purdie (6)
Cairn Primary School, Maybole

My First Acrostic - Southern Scotland Inspirations

Me!

E mily is my name and
M y favourite friend
I s Cassi and I really
L ike playing with my friends
Y ou can come and play, if you like.

Emily Maxwell (7)
Cairn Primary School, Maybole

Me!

L ittle and smart
O ranges are my favourite fruit
G ood at writing and I like
A nimals
N ow I am seven.

Logan McClounie (7)
Cairn Primary School, Maybole

My First Acrostic - Southern Scotland Inspirations

Me!

S o, I'm Sophie and I am great
O n Monday, Mrs Owens is great
P eople are nice to me
H elpful and kind to people
I am nice to my friends
E mily is nice to me!

Sophie Hearton (7)
Cairn Primary School, Maybole

Me!

C hloe is my name
H elpful to my friends and I
L ike Sophie and Emily
O utside I like to play
E very day.

Chloe Gladstone (7)
Cairn Primary School, Maybole

My First Acrostic - Southern Scotland Inspirations

Me!

D ouglas is my name
O range is my favourite colour
U nkind to people, not me!
G ood at maths
L ovely writing
A nd hardworking
S uper cool, that's me!

Douglas Strachan (6)
Cairn Primary School, Maybole

Me!

C ool and smart
A nd I am nice and I
L ike working with Miss Wickman
U ntidy, that's not me!
M y friend is Logan.

Calum Murray (6)
Cairn Primary School, Maybole

My First Acrostic - Southern Scotland Inspirations

Me!

J ade is my name
A nd my friends are Emily, Steffi and Cassi
D ay after day I play tig
E very day.

Jade Hepburn (8)
Cairn Primary School, Maybole

Me!

B rown hair has Brooke and I have a
R ing too!
O nce, I was third in a race
O utside is the best!
K ind, I am very kind
E veryone loves me!

Brooke Watson (6)
Cairn Primary School, Maybole

My First Acrostic - Southern Scotland Inspirations

Me!

T ia is my name and I am a clever girl
I n class, my friends
A re Emily, Sophie and Cassi.

Tia McLanaghan (6)
Cairn Primary School, Maybole

Me!

H arry is a happy person
A nd I am the best at football
R eally good at
R unning to the ball and
Y elling!

Harry McKenna (6)
Cairn Primary School, Maybole

My First Acrostic - Southern Scotland Inspirations

My Name Poem

J oyful Jade is seven
A ll I like to eat is bread and jam
D ancing Jade is eco-friendly
E xcited Mum and Dad give me lots of pennies.

Jade Arthur (7)
Carnbroe Primary School, Coatbridge

My Name Poem

J umping Jessica is six
E co-Jessica
S ister Jessica
S porty Jessica
I n and out Jessica
C aring Jessica
A rty Jessica.

Jessica Dunion (6)
Carnbroe Primary School, Coatbridge

My First Acrostic - Southern Scotland Inspirations

My Name Poem

F unny Freya is six
R acing is my life
E co is my favourite
Y oghurt is a treat
A nd I also hate beans!

Freya Crawley (6)
Carnbroe Primary School, Coatbridge

My Name Poem

R esponsible Rachael is six
A rt's good
C aring for people
H appy girl
A ngry - never
E co-friendly
L ikes to say goodbye.

Rachael Mackay (6)
Carnbroe Primary School, Coatbridge

My First Acrostic - Southern Scotland Inspirations

My Name Poem

J oyful Justin is seven
U ntidy never
S ensible
T iny never
I ntelligent
N ice.

Justin Harvie (7)
Carnbroe Primary School, Coatbridge

My Name Poem

C raig is kind and
R esponsible
A re you a good footballer?
I am a good artist
G ood.

Craig Renicks (6)
Carnbroe Primary School, Coatbridge

My First Acrostic - Southern Scotland Inspirations

My Name Poem

C raig is good
R unning is good
A pples are good
I like shopping
G reen is a good colour.

Craig Kerr (7)
Carnbroe Primary School, Coatbridge

My Name Poem

L ollipops are the best
E ggs poached
W ishes are cool to me
I nnocent I am
S porty I am.

Lewis McKean (6)
Carnbroe Primary School, Coatbridge

My First Acrostic - Southern Scotland Inspirations

My Name Poem

J umpy Jonathan
O ld Jonathan is nice
N ice people like me
A aron is good at football
T he baby is happy
H appy Jonathan
A m a good boy
N o mums like beans.

Jonathan Grabiec (6)
Carnbroe Primary School, Coatbridge

My Name Poem

H appy Hannah is six
A rt's good
N ice girl
N ice and responsible
A pples are good
H elping Mum.

Hannah Dunion (6)
Carnbroe Primary School, Coatbridge

My First Acrostic - Southern Scotland Inspirations

My Name Poem

M eer Faysal always plays football
E xcited with my mum and dad
E xcited with my big sister and my big brother
R yan is good at football

F aysal always plays football at home
A aron is good at football
Y ou are going to the art room
S ean is good at football
A nd my best friend is Aaron and Sean
L ewis never plays football.

Meer Faysal Ahmed (6)
Carnbroe Primary School, Coatbridge

Dirt Bikes

D irt bikes are cool
I love going on the track
R iding dirt bikes is cool
T racks are cool

B ikes are awesome
I love dirt bikes
K arting is not my thing
E very time I go on, it is fast
S ometimes I go on it.

Cameron Bell (6)
Coaltown of Wemyss Primary School, Kirkcaldy

My First Acrostic - Southern Scotland Inspirations

Wild Animals

W ild animals are cool
I like animals
L ions are fierce animals
D ead animals will be extinct soon

A nother animal will attack another animal
N ight animals will come out at night
I nsects are cool
M aggots are cool
A nd ladybirds are red and black
L ike another animal which won't come out at night
S ome animals will come out at night.

Denni Brown (8)
Coaltown of Wemyss Primary School, Kirkcaldy

Me

E legant
M arvellous
I love my mum and dad
L ovely
Y ou are cool.

Emily Rose Dick (6)
Coaltown of Wemyss Primary School, Kirkcaldy

My First Acrostic - Southern Scotland Inspirations

Me

A dam likes a boat
D ad is nice
A nd also funny
M um makes pancakes.

Adam Dixon (5)
Coaltown of Wemyss Primary School, Kirkcaldy

Me

B en likes buggies
E very day I play with them
N ever stop

D ad always comes
R oaring and rumbling
Y es, I do like my fish
B en likes cars
U p goes the flag
R acing round the track
G iving people presents
H elping people.

Ben Dryburgh (6)
Coaltown of Wemyss Primary School, Kirkcaldy

My First Acrostic - Southern Scotland Inspirations

Me

E llie is five
L eah is my cousin
L aughing is good
I like lambs
E veryone is happy.

Ellie Fraser (5)
Coaltown of Wemyss Primary School, Kirkcaldy

Me

My mum likes me
And my dad likes me too
Reading is my favourite thing
It is fun when I play with my friends
Nobody hurts me
And I go to my nanna's for a sleepover.

Marina Hendren (6)
Coaltown of Wemyss Primary School, Kirkcaldy

My First Acrostic - Southern Scotland Inspirations

Fishing

F ix the maggots on the line
I caught lots of fish
S ea-blue and wavy
H e went to another place
I caught another fish
N ever again
G etting the fish ready to eat.

Connor MacCuish (7)
Coaltown of Wemyss Primary School, Kirkcaldy

Me

K ye is good
Y ou are friends
E ggs are cool.

Kye Pickard (5)
Coaltown of Wemyss Primary School, Kirkcaldy

My First Acrostic - Southern Scotland Inspirations

Reading

R eading is good
E njoying new books
A nd reading is funny
D ad likes reading
I love reading too
N icole doesn't like reading
G ive me books any day.

Erin Rhodes (7)
Coaltown of Wemyss Primary School, Kirkcaldy

Me

L uke is good
U mbrellas are cool
K ites are my favourite
E verybody likes me.

Luke Rolland (5)
Coaltown of Wemyss Primary School, Kirkcaldy

My First Acrostic - Southern Scotland Inspirations

Going To The Beach

G oing to the park
O n the chute I like to be
I look at the swings
N o one around
G o to school today

T o the park today
O r I will run

T oday I meet my friends
H e is angry
E veryone is nice to me

B ye-bye to you
E veryone is reading books
A re you hiding?
C ome see everyone
H e is hiding.

Molly Walker (5)
Coaltown of Wemyss Primary School, Kirkcaldy

Dancing

F reestyle is a type of dancing
R espectful is my teacher at dancing
E veryone likes her style
E veryone thinks she's good
S tyle is good
T ests are coming up at dancing
Y ear by year we get better
L earning to dance is fun
E verybody makes friends

D ancing is fantastic
A ll the girls like to dance
N obody is nasty
C areful everybody is
I n dancing, we always have music on
N obody shouts out
G irls love to dance all the time.

Rosie Walker (7)
Coaltown of Wemyss Primary School, Kirkcaldy

My First Acrostic - Southern Scotland Inspirations

Tutankhamun

T he forgotten tomb lay undiscovered
U ncovered stairway led to his tomb
T housands of objects were around his tomb
A rchaeologists discovered his tomb over 70 years ago
N ebkheperure is his fourth name
K ing Tutankhamun was buried in a secret room
H e was nine years old when he was crowned
A boy called Adam looks like Tutankhamun
M edjay guarded Tutankhamun's pyramid
U nder Tutankhamun's death mask is his mummified body
N o other king is as famous as him.

Adam Bruce Hart (7)
Dairsie Primary School, Cupar

Pyramid

P yramids are made of big, heavy stones
Y ellow pyramids are tall and sandy
R iver Nile floods
A ncient Egyptians are scared of the desert
M ummification preserves mummies
I nside the coffins are wrapped-up mummies
D eserts are scary because of the wild animals roaming around.

Kerri Stalker (7)
Dairsie Primary School, Cupar

My First Acrostic - Southern Scotland Inspirations

Pyramid

P yramids are made out of lime stone blocks
Y ellow pyramids are shaped in a triangle
R iver Nile is very long
A ll the big boats sail on the River Nile
M ummies are placed in coffins
I nside a pyramid is Tutankhamun
D eserts have lots of smooth, yellow sand.

Louise Moncrieff (6)
Dairsie Primary School, Cupar

Sphinx

S phinx guards the front of the biggest triangular pyramid
P haraoh rules the mighty kingdom
H ey, I think there is a hidden room beneath the enormous sphinx
I t is a half-man and lion
N ose shot off by the camouflaged army
X -ray for the bandaged mummies.

Lewis Moyes (7)
Dairsie Primary School, Cupar

My First Acrostic - Southern Scotland Inspirations

Egypt

E gypt is hot and sandy
G uards protected the pyramids
Y ellow sand everywhere in Egypt
P eople in Egypt were farmers
T he Nile is very long and goes through three countries.

David Reay (6)
Dairsie Primary School, Cupar

Nile River

N ile is the largest river in the world
I t flows all over Egypt
L ots of boats laden with cargo
E very boat was made with papyrus

R iver Nile is really long
I t is really deep
V illages are along the Nile's riverbank
E ach person drank from the river
R esevoirs they built to trap and hold floodwater.

Chrissy Newton-Sutherland (6)
Dairsie Primary School, Cupar

My First Acrostic - Southern Scotland Inspirations

All About Me!

C hild, I am a child
O n, my brain is on all the time
N umber seven, my age is seven
A ctive, I am active
L arge, I am the biggest in the class
L ittle, I am little, because the adults are bigger than me.

Conall Moyes Wallace (7)
Dalgety Bay Primary School, Dalgety Bay

All About Me!

H urt, sometimes I'm hurt
A rt, I like art
N ever, never want to do stuff
N ice, I am nice to people
A ngry, I am sometimes angry
H ere, I will always be here.

Hannah Eadie (6)
Dalgety Bay Primary School, Dalgety Bay

My First Acrostic - Southern Scotland Inspirations

All About Me!

A dorable, I am adorable
B usy, I am busy
B lue, I like blue
E xcellent, I am excellent at drawing
Y ellow, yellow is my favourite colour

K atie, Katie is my friend
E ating, I like eating
R ed, I like red
R ebecca, Rebecca is my friend.

Abbey Kerr (6)
Dalgety Bay Primary School, Dalgety Bay

All About Me!

J oe, Joe is my fish
A pples, apples are my favourite food
M ax, Max is my friend
I ndiana Jones, Indiana Jones is my favourite movie
E lephants, elephants are my favourite animal.

Jamie Dawson (7)
Dalgety Bay Primary School, Dalgety Bay

My First Acrostic - Southern Scotland Inspirations

All About Me!

Wellies, I wear wellies when it's raining
Idea, I have no idea
Lovely, it is a lovely day
Like, I like old keys
Inside, inside my house is my little brother
Animals, I like animals
Mum, my mum is having a baby.

William McPhee White (7)
Dalgety Bay Primary School, Dalgety Bay

All About Me!

T iger, my favourite animal is a tiger
I like picking apples
F unny, I am quite funny
F ish, I like fish
A bby is my friend
N ot, it is not a good day today
I have an apple tree
E ating, I like eating spaghetti.

Tiffanie McColl (7)
Dalgety Bay Primary School, Dalgety Bay

All About Me!

B rown, I have brown hair
E ggs, I like eggs
T eddy, I have a teddy
H annah, Hannah is my friend
A pples, I like apples
N oisy, I am noisy
Y oung, I am young.

Bethany Leitch (6)
Dalgety Bay Primary School, Dalgety Bay

All About Me!

R ed is my favourite colour
A nimals, I like koalas
C hloe is my friend
H annah is my best friend
E ggs, I eat eggs
L emon, I like lemon.

Rachel Rowntree (7)
Dalgety Bay Primary School, Dalgety Bay

All About Me!

S hort, I am short
E ggs, I like eating eggs
A pples, I like apples
N ext, I like getting my clothes from Next.

Sean Bartholomew (6)
Dalgety Bay Primary School, Dalgety Bay

All About Me!

R ed tongue
Y ellow
A pples
N ice

D inosaurs.

Ryan Daley (6)
Dalgety Bay Primary School, Dalgety Bay

My First Acrostic - Southern Scotland Inspirations

All About Me!

R ight, I am always right
Y oghurt, I like yoghurt
A pples, I like apples
N o, I say no!

Ryan Harrison (6)
Dalgety Bay Primary School, Dalgety Bay

All About Me!

R yan H is my best friend
Y esterday, yesterday I went to see a T-rex
A untie, I wish I had an auntie
N ice, I am nice to everyone

A ngel, I am a little angel.

Ryan Aitken (6)
Dalgety Bay Primary School, Dalgety Bay

My First Acrostic - Southern Scotland Inspirations

All About Me!

J am, I like jam on my toast
O ranges, I like eating oranges
H ouse, I play in my house
N umbers, I think numbers are easy.

John Ardila-Neville (6)
Dalgety Bay Primary School, Dalgety Bay

All About Me!

S mart, I am smart
A bbey K, Abbey K is my friend
C hloe, Chloe is my friend
I ndigo, indigo is my favourite colour.

Saci Marton (6)
Dalgety Bay Primary School, Dalgety Bay

All About Me!

M ax is my name
A pples, I like apples
X -ray, I have never had an X-ray before.

Max Johnston (7)
Dalgety Bay Primary School, Dalgety Bay

All About Me!

L ovely, I am lovely
E ating, I like eating apples
A rt, I like doing art
H ats, I like wearing hats.

Leah Murray (6)
Dalgety Bay Primary School, Dalgety Bay

My First Acrostic - Southern Scotland Inspirations

All About Me!

A lright, I am alright
N ine, nine is my second favourite number
D inosaurs, I like dinosaurs
R ed, red is my third favourite colour
E ggs, I like eggs
W hite, white is my second favourite colour.

Andrew Elliott (6)
Dalgety Bay Primary School, Dalgety Bay

All About Me!

R aces, I like races
O ops! I say, 'Oops,' because I fall
S cott, Scott is my brother
S tar Wars, I like Star Wars.

Ross Williamson (7)
Dalgety Bay Primary School, Dalgety Bay

My First Acrostic - Southern Scotland Inspirations

All About Me!

J og, I jog
A pples, I like apples
M ad, I am mad sometimes
E xcellent, I am excellent
S hort, I am short.

James Uphill (6)
Dalgety Bay Primary School, Dalgety Bay

All About Me!

A pples, I love apples
B lue, I like the colour blue
B all, I have a purple ball
Y ellow, yellow is my favourite colour.

Abby Paveling (6)
Dalgety Bay Primary School, Dalgety Bay

My First Acrostic - Southern Scotland Inspirations

All About Me!

E ilidh is my friend
M iss Robertson is lovely
M agic, I am magic
A bby is my friend.

Emma Stuart (6)
Dalgety Bay Primary School, Dalgety Bay

All About Me!

E nergy
W hoops!
A ngry
N ice

L ucky
O nly
G ood
A ctive
N early seven!

Ewan Logan (6)
Dalgety Bay Primary School, Dalgety Bay

My First Acrostic - Southern Scotland Inspirations

All About Me!

C lever, I am clever
H elping, I am helping
L ittle, I have a little sister
O range, orange is my favourite colour
E mma, Emma is my friend

M argaret, Margaret is my mum's mum
E ilidh, Eilidh is my friend
G reen, green is my favourite colour
E wan, Ewan is my big brother
N aughty, I am not naughty

D ad, I have a dad
O ut, I like playing outside
M um, I have a mum
I like owls
N ice, I am nice
Y o-Yo, my nickname is Yo-Yo.

Chloe Megen Dominy (6)
Dalgety Bay Primary School, Dalgety Bay

Nessie

N essie nibbles at fish
E ats fish and frogs and tadpoles
S ees rocks and mountains and cliffs
S mells people on horses
I s big and scary
E njoys cows and calves for tea!

Naomi Calley (6)
Dalry Primary School, Dalry

My First Acrostic - Southern Scotland Inspirations

Nessie

N ibbles at food and crackers
E ats frogs and fish
S ees people and animals
S mells fish and clothes
I s a big, scary monster
E njoys eating people and animals.

Travis Blakely (6)
Dalry Primary School, Dalry

Nessie

N eeds water
E ats fish, plants, apples and frogs
S ees people and rock
S mells funny, like fish smoke and dirt
I s a big, scary monster
E xciting and looks all green.

Andrew Allan (7)
Dalry Primary School, Dalry

My First Acrostic - Southern Scotland Inspirations

Nessie

N essie likes to go to play
E ats fish and seaweed
S ees people
S ees clothes
I s a monster
E njoys playing with children.

Luke Stalker (6)
Dalry Primary School, Dalry

Nessie

N essie eats fish and drinks water
E njoys staying in Scotland
S cary monster
S houts loud
I s nice
E ats people.

Cameron Shaw (6)
Dalry Primary School, Dalry

My First Acrostic - Southern Scotland Inspirations

Nessie

N eeds water and sunshine
E ats fish and squid
S ees people and waves
S mells funny, like frogs
I s a big monster
E njoys staying in Scotland.

Isabelle Hill (6)
Dalry Primary School, Dalry

Nessie

N eeds water and fish
E ats fish and people
S ees waves and fish
S mells like fish and squid
I s a big, scary monster
E njoys staying in Scotland.

Adam Gilbert (7)
Dalry Primary School, Dalry

My First Acrostic - Southern Scotland Inspirations

Nessie

N ice and kind and helpful
E ats fish and drinks water
S ees fish and seagulls
S mells like fish and plants
I s funny and good
E njoys sleeping and laughing.

Marni Caig (7)
Dalry Primary School, Dalry

Nessie

N essie likes food and water
E ats fish and seaweed
S mells like people and sleep
S he likes eels and squid
I s enjoying swimming
E njoys eating.

Amy Murphy (6)
Dalry Primary School, Dalry

Nessie

N ever eats people and is nice
E ats fish and people
S ees children playing near
S mells fish and smoke near
I s big and green
E njoys staying in Scotland.

Abigail Campbell (6)
Dalry Primary School, Dalry

Nessie

N essie needs water
E ats fish and squid
S ees people and children
S wims good
I see Nessie and he is green
E njoys staying in Scotland.

Dale Martin (6)
Dalry Primary School, Dalry

My First Acrostic - Southern Scotland Inspirations

Nessie

N essie is nice
E ats fish
S ees rabbits
S mells smoke
I s a big, scary monster
E ats plants.

Jade McCafferty (6)
Dalry Primary School, Dalry

Nessie

N eeds food and water
E ats fish and frogs
S ees people
S ees oceans
I s looking at me
E njoys swimming.

Eilidh Stewart (6)
Dalry Primary School, Dalry

My First Acrostic - Southern Scotland Inspirations

Nessie

N eeds water
E ats fish
S ees children
S ees Scotland
I s a big monster
E njoys staying in Scotland.

Jenna Russell (6)
Dalry Primary School, Dalry

Nessie

N essie is nice to people
E ats fish and boats
S ees hills and rocks and people
S mells fish and people
I s a big, scary monster
E njoys staying in Scotland.

Brooke Neill (7)
Dalry Primary School, Dalry

My First Acrostic - Southern Scotland Inspirations

The Clown

C olourful hair and spinning bow tie
L aughing because a clown is squirting water at me
O h! He throws a pie at me
W alking along a tightrope
N ow he falls off into a bucket of goo!

Jennifer Boyd (5)
Houston Primary School, Houston

The Clown

C razy clown
L eaping through the air
O n a poor mouse
W ow! The mouse wriggles
N ow he throws a custard pie.

Isaac Nayar (6)
Houston Primary School, Houston

My First Acrostic - Southern Scotland Inspirations

The Clown

C olourful baggy trousers
L aughing when they fall down
O h, no! Big, spotty underpants
W obbling on a unicycle
N ow he falls off!

Innes Durrant (6)
Houston Primary School, Houston

The Clown

C razy clowns throwing pies
L ands on my face
O h no!
W ater's splashing on my head
N ow I push him into a bucket of water.

Lewis McGeachin (6)
Houston Primary School, Houston

My First Acrostic - Southern Scotland Inspirations

The Clown

C olourful clown climbing a ladder
L aughing when his trousers fall down
O h no! He falls off the tightrope
W et slime splashes all over me
N ow I'm laughing!

Catherine Abdallah (5)
Houston Primary School, Houston

The Clown

C an you hear the old clown car?
L aughing when the doors fall off!
O h! An elephant sits on the car
W alking along a tightrope
N ow the clown falls onto a pot of green goo!

Amy Lawson (5)
Houston Primary School, Houston

My First Acrostic - Southern Scotland Inspirations

The Clown

C ustard pies
L anding on me
O i! Mr Clown
W hat a silly clown
N ot on me!

Abby Birrell (5)
Houston Primary School, Houston

The Clown

C urious clowns up to mischief!
L ooking for pranks to play on people
O h no! He squirts me with his flower!
W earing his colourful, curly wig
N ow he is dancing with his friends.

Leah Feely (5)
Houston Primary School, Houston

My First Acrostic - Southern Scotland Inspirations

The Clown

C olourful, flowery top
L aughing and giggling
O ops! He fell over
W atch him juggle
N ever trust a clown!

Robyn Stirling (5)
Houston Primary School, Houston

The Clown

C urious clowns up to mischief
L ooking for pranks to play
O h, no! He squirts me
W earing his colourful, curly wig
N ow he is dancing with his friends.

Daniel Hatfield (5)
Houston Primary School, Houston

My First Acrostic - Southern Scotland Inspirations

The Clown

C olourful clown
L anding in water
O h no! Water, silly clown!
W ater, water, everywhere!
N ot a drop on me!

Hannah Robertson (5)
Houston Primary School, Houston

The Clown

C lowns are on the rope
L ook at them juggling
O n a long, blue rope
W hat a big surprise!
N ot a wobble at all!

Katy Mitchell (5)
Houston Primary School, Houston

My First Acrostic - Southern Scotland Inspirations

The Clown

C olourful clown
L aughing at me
O ver a bike he falls
'W ow!' he shouts
'N ot a mouse!'

Harris Cunningham (5)
Houston Primary School, Houston

The Clown

C razy clowns
L aughing
O h, no!
W atch out! An elephant sat on the car
N othing left but a steering wheel!

Louis Jeffrey (5)
Houston Primary School, Houston

My First Acrostic - Southern Scotland Inspirations

Bethany

B ethany likes sweets
E ating pizza
T alks to anybody
H as Barbie toys
A pples are my favourite
N ever chat
Y ellow is my favourite colour.

Bethany Catchpole (6)
Macmerry Primary School, Macmerry

Niamh

N iamh is mad at skipping
I s good at football
A lways chats
M ad about drawing
H appy to make friends.

Niamh Renwick (6)
Macmerry Primary School, Macmerry

My First Acrostic - Southern Scotland Inspirations

Zara

Z ara likes football
A football game is fun
R is for my dad's name, Russel
A trampoline is fun.

Zara Johnston (6)
Macmerry Primary School, Macmerry

Loch Lomond

L och Lomond has a small beach
O n the banks, it's like the seaside
C an you swim in the pool?
H ow would you get there?

L ovely golf course there
O n the tennis court, it is fun
M ost tourists come to see the loch
O n the beach, it is fun
N ow you can hear boats
D o you know how to get there?

Ruby Stewart (8)
Markinch Primary School, Markinch

My First Acrostic - Southern Scotland Inspirations

Orkney

O rkney is a brilliant place
R ide on a ferry to get there
K ids can play at the play park
N ear the sea there is a stone called the Ring of Brodgar
E verybody is so nice at the campsite
Y ou will love it - bye!

Aislinn Wilkie (7)
Markinch Primary School, Markinch

Edinburgh

E dinburgh is a great place for a holiday
D elightful zoo in Edinburgh
I t's a great place
N ip over the Forth Road Bridge
B ig shops in Edinburgh
U nder Edinburgh is the dungeon
R oyalty used to live there
G o to Edinburgh to see historical sights
H ope to see you in Edinburgh!

Rebeka Korosi (8)
Markinch Primary School, Markinch

My First Acrostic - Southern Scotland Inspirations

Dunfermline

D unfermline is an historic place
U nder the abbey is Robert Bruce's grave
N ame a place and it's there
F amilies play in Pittencrief Park
E ver been to Dunfermline?
R ide in your car
M ake it fun for all the family, by going to Pittencrief Park
L et the historic places take you back in time
I t is a fantastic place at the Abbey
N ow you can see the fantastic places
E nd your journey fascinated!

Liana Fergus (8)
Markinch Primary School, Markinch

Dysart

D ysart is a great place to visit
Y ou can go to the seaside
S andy beaches, where you can build sandcastles
A t Dysart, there is a harbour and some seashells
R ide to Dysart in your car
T here is lots of stuff to do!

Nadia Ali (8)
Markinch Primary School, Markinch

My First Acrostic - Southern Scotland Inspirations

Leven

L even is a good place to visit
E ven they have a big pool
V ery good parks to play in
E ven they have shops in Leven
N early all the shops have good stuff in, like food, toys, books, clothes and drinks.

Morgan Birrell (8)
Markinch Primary School, Markinch

Dysart

D ysart is fun to go to
Y ou can go to the beach
S o will you go? No?
A harbour master's home is there
R eal seals are on the beach
T ry to go there if you can.

Andrew Milne (8)
Markinch Primary School, Markinch

My First Acrostic - Southern Scotland Inspirations

Dunfermline

D unfermline is a fantastic place
U sually you can go to Dunfermline Abbey and you can go inside and see a real golden grave of King Robert the Bruce
N ew things are in the Abbey
F orever a good place to go
E ver been to Dunfermline?
R obert the Bruce was very old when he died
M y dad and I love it
L ovely place to go
I nteresting things to see
N ice shops and parks to visit
E njoy your trip!

Kayley McKenzie (8)
Markinch Primary School, Markinch

Oban

O n the beach you can see Mull
B urger shop is next to Tesco
A nd there is a picture house
N ew fishing boats look cool.

Ryan Wilson (7)
Markinch Primary School, Markinch

My First Acrostic - Southern Scotland Inspirations

St Andrews

S t Andrews is a fantastic place
T here are lots of things to do

A castle sits beside the golf course
N ew things are in the castle
D own on the beach you can find pretty shells
R ocks are beside the beach
E ver been to St Andrews?
W onderful place to go
S een the golf course?

Charlotte Mackenzie (8)
Markinch Primary School, Markinch

Oban

O ban is a great place
B oats are docked in Oban harbour
A burger shop is there
N ew colosseum has just been made.

Kyle Anderson (8)
Markinch Primary School, Markinch

My First Acrostic - Southern Scotland Inspirations

Leven

L even is fun
E very Wednesday I go to the pool for swimming lessons
V ery often, the tide is in on the beach
E verybody should go to Leven
N ow Leven is a great place to go.

Liam Gregory (8)
Markinch Primary School, Markinch

Markinch

M arkinch is in Fife
A nd there are three parks
R ide your bike and look at nature
K irkaldy is near Markinch
I n Markinch you can go to the park
N ear the school is Bowling Green Road
C hurch bells ring on Sundays
H ope you can visit!

Aidan Duff (8)
Markinch Primary School, Markinch

My First Acrostic - Southern Scotland Inspirations

Markinch

M arkinch is a good place to stay
A nd you can go to the shops
R ide to Markinch on the bus
K eep coming to Markinch Highland Games
I n Markinch you can go to the park
N ice school for your children
C hildren play safely in the park
H ope you come soon.

Matthew Barrie (8)
Markinch Primary School, Markinch

Loch Lomond

L och Lomond is a fun place to go
O n Loch Lomond is a good place for boat trips
C an you come and see the loch?
H ow will you get there?

L eave your pets at home
O nly for a short while
M ake a picnic
O r go to a restaurant
N ice loch views
D on't forget to go!

Ryan Todd (7)
Markinch Primary School, Markinch

My First Acrostic - Southern Scotland Inspirations

Rowley

R owley is my second name
O ctopuses are my favourite fish
W ario is my favourite character
L otus cars are the fastest
E lephants never forget
Y ellow is my favourite colour.

Jay Rowley (7)
St Bernard's Primary School, Coatbridge

Summer

S ummer is my favourite season
U mbrellas are not needed in summer
M y mum buys me pretty dresses in summer
M y garden is my favourite place
E ating ice lollies cools me down
R ejoice in summer!

Necole Lannigan (7)
St Bernard's Primary School, Coatbridge

My First Acrostic - Southern Scotland Inspirations

Jordan

J ordan is my name and I like football
O ranges are my favourite fruit
R ipples are my favourite chocolate
D ogs are my favourite pet
A pples are my second favourite fruit
N ovels are the stories that my group read.

Jordan McCann (7)
St Bernard's Primary School, Coatbridge

Kieran

K icking a ball makes me happy
I love football
E veryone comes to watch me play
R ight wing is where I play
A mazing football is the best
N ow we have to play to win.

Kieran McGrath (8)
St Bernard's Primary School, Coatbridge

My First Acrostic - Southern Scotland Inspirations

Duffy

D rawing is my favourite thing
U nder my bed I have lots of toys
F ingers help me count
F ootball is a good sport
Y ellow is my favourite colour.

Aidan Duffy (7)
St Bernard's Primary School, Coatbridge

Rocco

R eading is fun
O range is a great colour
C ounting is fun
C ooking is fun
O ctopus is a fish.

Rocco Rossetti (7)
St Bernard's Primary School, Coatbridge

My First Acrostic - Southern Scotland Inspirations

Martin

M y name is Bethany
A pples are my favourite fruit
R hys is my little brother
T ony is my dad's name
I am seven years old
N ibbles is my hamster's name.

Bethany Martin (7)
St Bernard's Primary School, Coatbridge

Lily

L ily is my name
I am seven years old
L iam, Bethany, Necole and Chloe are my friends
Y ellow and pink are my favourite colours.

Lily McGuire (7)
St Bernard's Primary School, Coatbridge

My First Acrostic - Southern Scotland Inspirations

Cullen

C ool at playing pool
U nbelievable at football
L anguage is fun
L iam and Jay are my best friends
E aster is my favourite time of year
N o one can spell my name.

Andrew Cullen (8)
St Bernard's Primary School, Coatbridge

Liam

L ooking at cars is cool
I have a car and it is a BMW
A fter I learn to drive, I would like to get a Subaru
M y name is Liam and I like cars.

Liam Hamilton (7)
St Bernard's Primary School, Coatbridge

My First Acrostic - Southern Scotland Inspirations

Angel

A m kind to my brother
N ew toys at Christmas
G ood at making a story
E mpty tummy yesterday
L ike sweets all the time.

Angel McIlhatton (7)
St Marie's Primary School, Kirkcaldy

Josh Leblanc

J elly is the best
O ranges are too
S uper writer
H ates school

L ove pizza
E xcellent at talking
B est writer
L azy all the time
A lways playing on the PS2
N ever loud
C ounting is easy.

Josh Leblanc (7)
St Marie's Primary School, Kirkcaldy

My First Acrostic - Southern Scotland Inspirations

Bethany Kinnaird

B oring person
E xcellent at writing
T otally good
H appy all the time
A lright
N uts all the time
Y ellow is my favourite colour

K ind and caring
I ce cream cools me down
N uts all the time
N ice all the time
A ble to do anything
I cing is cool
R iding a horse is fun
D ad I love.

Bethany Kinnaird (7)
St Marie's Primary School, Kirkcaldy

Calum

C alum likes football
A lways scores goals
L ikes to play computer games
U ntil it's time for bed
M ario Kart is the best.

Calum Robertson (7)
St Marie's Primary School, Kirkcaldy

My First Acrostic - Southern Scotland Inspirations

Megan Rae

M akes lots of mistakes
E xcellent at art
G ood girl
A good writer
N ever a bad girl

R eally nice
A mazing at reading
E xcellent at making music.

Megan Rae (7)
St Marie's Primary School, Kirkcaldy

Rhys

R eally fun
H i, I am always happy
Y oung and funny
S uper Mario is my favourite game.

Rhys Maksymuik (7)
St Marie's Primary School, Kirkcaldy

My First Acrostic - Southern Scotland Inspirations

Ricky

R aces
I like ice cream
C olouring is my favourite
K etchup on my chips
Y oghurt makes me grow.

Ricky Keatings (7)
St Marie's Primary School, Kirkcaldy

Andrew

A nnoying a lot
N ippy a lot
D estroys my brother's toys
R eally good at art
E normous for my age
W ednesday is the worst day of my life.

Andrew Doherty (7)
St Marie's Primary School, Kirkcaldy

My First Acrostic - Southern Scotland Inspirations

Rachel

R eading is my favourite thing
A lways angry with my little sister
C areful with my friends
H appy sometimes with my big brother
E asy I find school
L azy girl at home.

Rachel McGregor (7)
St Marie's Primary School, Kirkcaldy

Olivia Taylor

O ranges are very nice
L ives in a house
I ce cream is my favourite
V ery nice
I nvite friends to stay
A pples are my favourite food

T aylor from High School Musical, I like
A ngel is my friend
Y oghurt is nice
L oves buying clothes
O ranges are nice
R osy is my best friend.

Olivia Taylor (7)
St Marie's Primary School, Kirkcaldy

My First Acrostic - Southern Scotland Inspirations

Kara Gallacher

K ind and careful
A ngry with my sisters
R eally young
A lways funny

G lad all the time
A nts I like
L ucky girl
L ovely girl
A nimals I like
C akes I love
H air is dirty blonde
E arly for parties
R aces are good and fun.

Kara Gallacher (7)
St Marie's Primary School, Kirkcaldy

Sophie Hockham

S o helpful with things
O nly special on my birthday
P ain in the neck
H ate school all the time
I ce cream is good
E at good food

H ate tigers a lot
O nly good at writing
C uddles from my mum and dad
K ind to people
H am is good to eat
A pples are good
M y mum is great.

Sophie Hockham (7)
St Marie's Primary School, Kirkcaldy

My First Acrostic - Southern Scotland Inspirations

Kirstin Anderson

K ind and helpful
I nsane at home
R eally excitable on my birthday
S uper writer at school
T errible at maths
I ncredible at gymnastics
N ew stuff all the time

A lot of apples I eat
N uts are yuck
D igs in my dad's pocket
E xitable with my dad
R eally weird
S ings at home
O n the weekend plays with pals
N ight-time is boring.

Kirstin Anderson (7)
St Marie's Primary School, Kirkcaldy

Joseph Ciaraldi

J oyful sometimes
O nly special on my birthday
S o special
E xcited all the time
P ain in the neck
H elpful all the time

C ream is nice
I ce cream is nice too
A pples are good
R ays in my house are soft
A lways nosy
L ambs are good
D estroying stuff is bad
I ce is cold.

Joseph Ciaraldi (7)
St Marie's Primary School, Kirkcaldy

My First Acrostic - Southern Scotland Inspirations

Sharks

S harks are evil
H urt fish
A ngry
R azor-sharp teeth
K illers.

Michael Kelly, Andrew Burns (6) & Luca Faccenda (7)
St Mary's Primary School, Largs

Fish

F ish are shiny
I t eats plants
S cared of sharks
H ave eyes at the side.

Amy Mullen & Hannah Muir (6)
St Mary's Primary School, Largs

My First Acrostic - Southern Scotland Inspirations

Fish

F ish are delicate creatures
I t eats plants
S wims in the deep blue sea
H ides from the big sharks.

Megan Pratt & Megan Ward (6)
St Mary's Primary School, Largs

Sharks

S harks eat fish
H appy when they see fish
A ngry face when fish get away
R rrrr, swim
K illers, danger!

Daniel McGowan & Lauren McCaig (6)
St Mary's Primary School, Largs

My First Acrostic - Southern Scotland Inspirations

Sharks

S harks eat fish
H yper speed is the speed they go
A ngry animals
R azor-sharp teeth
K ings of the oceans.

Megan Kelly (6) & Christopher McKinlay (7)
St Mary's Primary School, Largs

Fish

F riendly
I t eats plants
S wims in and out of holes
H ides from sharks.

Brooke Perry & Kian Murdoch (6)
St Mary's Primary School, Largs

My First Acrostic - Southern Scotland Inspirations

Fish

F ins are wavy
I t eats plants
S cuttling in the sea
H uddling with friends.

Stan Rodger & Anna Capocchi (6)
St Mary's Primary School, Largs

Egyptians

E gyptologists are cool
G ods and goddesses
Y ou're sailing down the Nile
P erfect mummification
T ombs are beautiful
I n Egypt it is very hot
A mazing mummy
N ice flatbread
S carab beetle gives you luck.

Alyx Mackie (7)
St Mary's Primary School, Lanark

My First Acrostic - Southern Scotland Inspirations

Egyptians

E xcellent mummies
G ods and goddesses
Y ummy flatbread
P haraohs have servants
T he Sphinx was built to protect the pyramids
I t is exciting when you look inside a pyramid
A nubis is a god
N efertiti was a queen
S un god, Ra.

Chloe Marshall (7)
St Mary's Primary School, Lanark

Egyptians

E gyptians built the pyramids
G iza has great and grand pyramids
Y ummy flatbread
P yramids of Giza
T utankhamun is a pharaoh
I msety-contained liver
A ncient Egypt is an old story
N ile has lots of crocodiles
S carab beetles give good luck.

Tové McCarthy (7)
St Mary's Primary School, Lanark

My First Acrostic - Southern Scotland Inspirations

Egyptians

E xciting hieroglyphics
G reat Giza pyramids
Y ummy flatbread
P yramids are bright
T utankhamun's death mask
I msety contains the liver
A ncient Egyptians
N efertiti is the most loveliest queen
S carab beetles are black.

Kerry Noble (6)
St Mary's Primary School, Lanark

Egyptians

E gyptians write on papyrus
G ods protect the Earth
Y achts go up the River Nile
P apyrus is the Egyptians' paper
T utankhamun has four sarcophagi
I ncredible Giza
A mazing pharaohs
N asty pharaohs
S ucceeding Egyptians.

Mark Scott (6)
St Mary's Primary School, Lanark

Egyptians

E gypt has the longest river
G reat pharaohs are cool
Y ummy mummy
P yramids are very wonderful
T ombs are famous
I n the night, tombs get robbed
A ncient Egypt
N othing is better than Egypt
S ickles are great.

Erin Snow (7)
St Mary's Primary School, Lanark

Egyptians

E gypt is a cool land
G iza has great pyramids
Y ellow is the sand's colour
P haraohs are wicked
T ombs have mummies in them
I n the pyramids there is gold
A ncient Egypt
N obody climbed on the Sphinx
S ickles have sharp ends.

Mark Bustard (6)
St Mary's Primary School, Lanark

My First Acrostic - Southern Scotland Inspirations

Egyptians

E gyptians have yellow sand
G reat pyramid of Giza
Y ou are sailing down the River Nile
P yramids are protected
T ombs are spooky, tombs are dark
I msety-contained liver
A ncient Egyptians
N ever climb in tombs
S un god, Ra.

Jordan Oakes (6)
St Mary's Primary School, Lanark

Egyptians

E xcellent Egypt
G reat Giza
Y ellow pyramids are bright
P haraohs are cool
T utankhamun
I sis
A ncient Egypt
N ile
S phinx.

Lewis Dowie (7)
St Mary's Primary School, Lanark

Egyptians

E gyptians wrapped mummies
G iza
Y ellow flatbread
P yramids were built by slaves
T ombs had great statues
I msety-contained liver
A mummy got out of his tomb
N ile
S phinx protects the pyramids.

Tanya Brennan (6)
St Mary's Primary School, Lanark

Egyptians

E xciting Egypt
G reat pyramids of Giza
Y achts carried the Egyptians
P haraohs wore very cool things
T hoth was the god of scribes
I nside a tomb I saw a mummy
A long time ago the Egyptians came
N o one was above the pharaohs
S laves were rewarded if they did well.

Sam McFadyen (7)
St Mary's Primary School, Lanark

My First Acrostic - Southern Scotland Inspirations

Egyptians

E xciting gods
G eb is the god of Earth
Y ou are entering the past of Egypt
P apyrus is Egyptian paper
T hoth is the god of learning and scribes
I msety is one of the jars
A nubis is the god of the underworld
N ile is the longest river
S carab beetles.

John Gair (7)
St Mary's Primary School, Lanark

Egyptians

E gyptian gods are cool
G reat pyramids of Giza
Y ou are entering the past
P yramids are fab
T hoth, the god of learning and scribes
I sis, the goddess of protection
A nubis, the god of the dead
N ut, the god of the sky
S eth, the god of chaos.

Benji MacDonald (7)
St Mary's Primary School, Lanark

My First Acrostic - Southern Scotland Inspirations

Egyptians

E gypt has mummies kept in tombs
G reat pyramids
Y ummy mummy was in the newspaper
P yramids
T he Sphinx is cool
I ncredible mummies
A mazing facts about Egypt
N ile
S phinx.

Rachel Donnachie (6)
St Mary's Primary School, Lanark

Egyptians

E gypt is a desert
G reat pyramids of Giza
Y ummy flatbread
P haraohs are great
T he Nile is the longest river in the world
I n ancient Egypt, a boy pharaoh lived
A rchaeologists discovered tombs
N efertiti was a queen
S phinx and pharaohs.

Enya McKnight (6)
St Mary's Primary School, Lanark

My First Acrostic - Southern Scotland Inspirations

Egyptians

E gyptians built pyramids
G ods and goddesses
Y ellow pyramids
P haraohs wear crowns
T asting flatbread
I n Egypt it's hot
A mulets are spiky
N efertiti
S un god, Ra.

Holly Smith (6)
St Mary's Primary School, Lanark

My Family

M um
Y ou love me

F un
A llan
M y brother
I s fun
L ove you
Y ou're great.

Cameron Dickie (5)
St Mary's Primary School, Lanark

My First Acrostic - Southern Scotland Inspirations

My Family

M ummy is very kind
Y ou love me

F ar away Daddy
A bsolutely perfect
M agnificent brother
I s fab
L auren
Y ou cook well.

Olivia Ferguson (5)
St Mary's Primary School, Lanark

My Family

M ummy
Y ou're the best

F avourite
A nd Daddy
M y favourite family
I s fun
L ove you
Y ou cook well.

Keva Culkin (5)
St Mary's Primary School, Lanark

My First Acrostic - Southern Scotland Inspirations

My Family

M y mum is nice
Y es, I love you

F avourite brother
A nd Dad
M y Ma
I love you
L ove you
Y ou love me.

Leoni Kay Fletcher (6)
St Mary's Primary School, Lanark

My Family

M atthew
Y oung brother

F avourite brother
A nd Dad
M y mum
I love you
L auren
Y ou love me.

Daniel Balmer (5)
St Mary's Primary School, Lanark

My First Acrostic - Southern Scotland Inspirations

Rainforest

R ain pours down, every drop goes by
A cheetah runs faster than a motorbike
I n the rainforest slugs and lots more are there
N othing is slower than a sloth
F lying squirrels bounce from tree to tree
O wl butterflies freak me out
R oar goes the tiger, you are so scared
E piphyte is green and red
S ome lizards such as skinks, make their tails fall off
   if they are attacked
T ime for some fun exploring here
S unday is fun to come to see the rainforest.

Shannon McCutcheon (7)
Sheuchan Primary School, Stranraer

Niall

N ice Niall
I like ice skating
A pril is my birthday
L oves to eat ice cream
L ouie is my friend's little brother.

Niall Slavin (7)
Sheuchan Primary School, Stranraer

My First Acrostic - Southern Scotland Inspirations

Brook

B rook likes to play football
R aindrops are my favourite sweets
O range is my favourite fruit
O range is my best colour
K ey to go to the door.

Brook Chandler (7)
Sheuchan Primary School, Stranraer

Joel

J oel likes football and
O ranges, he always looks
E xcellent and
L oves his wee brother.

Joel Thomson (8)
Sheuchan Primary School, Stranraer

My First Acrostic - Southern Scotland Inspirations

Easter

E aster is a time to remember what Jesus did for the world
A lways remember Jesus loves us
S on of God
T he tomb held Jesus
E aster is a time to
R emember Jesus!

Dawn Wyllie (7)
Sheuchan Primary School, Stranraer

Rainforests

R ainforests have lots of animals
A nd plants and trees
I n the rainforest you can get 2% light
N early every animal eats meat
F orest floors are dark and gloomy
O yster mushrooms grow on the
R ainforest floor
E piphyte is a type of flower
S quirrel monkeys live in the trees
T apirs eat lots of insects.

Emma Smith (8)
Sheuchan Primary School, Stranraer

My First Acrostic - Southern Scotland Inspirations

Robbie

R obbie is my name
O ranges are my favourite fruit
B obby and Brody are my pets
B ut they are quite big
I like playing with Gordon
E veryone likes me.

Robbie Wilson (8)
Sheuchan Primary School, Stranraer

Rainforests

R ainforests
A re being destroyed
I n America and
N orth West America
F armers are burning them
O r growing crops
R ainforests are dying
E very second a
S trong, big
T ree falls
S uddenly down and dies.

Gordon Forbes & Lewis McCamon (7)
Sheuchan Primary School, Stranraer

My First Acrostic - Southern Scotland Inspirations

Callum

C allum
A ctive
L ucky at football
L ikes to eat bananas
U pstairs
M um thinks I'm funny.

Callum Lees (7)
Sheuchan Primary School, Stranraer

Winter

Winter icicles hanging from the window ledge
I ced shortbread sitting in a packet
N ight-time with a really bright star
T hick trees with bare branches
E veryone excited lying in their beds
R obins sitting in trees.

Grace Peacock (6)
Towerbank Primary School, Edinburgh

My First Acrostic - Southern Scotland Inspirations

Winter

When it is winter there is ice on the water
I cicles hanging from the doors
N ice snow dropping from the sky
T he leaves fall off the trees
E veryone likes playing in the snow
R obins are eating good food in somebody's garden.

Hugo Boland (7)
Towerbank Primary School, Edinburgh

Winter

W hite snow is falling from the sky
I ce is so slippery that you can do penguin slides
N ice elves give the toys they have made to Santa
T hick is the white snow that falls from the sky
E xcitement runs through my body on the 24th of December
R obins and animals can't find their food.

Alexander Marriott (6)
Towerbank Primary School, Edinburgh

My First Acrostic - Southern Scotland Inspirations

Winter

W hite snow falls to the ground; people have snowball fights
I cicles hanging off the windows
N ight-time, the sun has gone, everyone is sleeping
T he thick snow on the ground is crunchy
E veryone screams with joy
R obins come out in the winter.

Eva Donnelly (6)
Towerbank Primary School, Edinburgh

Winter

W hite winter
I love the snow
N ever-ending sleep
T hank goodness it's Christmas
E vergreen plants grow
R un in the snow.

Hamish Martin (7)
Towerbank Primary School, Edinburgh

My First Acrostic - Southern Scotland Inspirations

Winter

W hite, thick snow falls from the sky
I ce is all over the puddles and Jack Frost was out at night
N ight-time is quiet, I never notice that there are icicles
  on my window
T ime to put up your stocking
E veryone is celebrating
R ed nose flashes at my window.

Jorgey Scott-Learmonth (6)
Towerbank Primary School, Edinburgh

My Friend

C reative Cameron is really cool
A nd adventurous and brave
M ighty and so strong, he can lift an
E lephant, he is faster than a
R ally race car, so he'll beat you
O utrageous in every way
N obody is faster . . . wow!

Gavin Neil (7)
Whitecrook Primary School, Clydebank

My First Acrostic - Southern Scotland Inspirations

My Friend

G iggling Gavin is
A lways the coolest, he
V anishes under a magic cloak
I s he a wizard?
N obody knows!

Cameron Henderson (6)
Whitecrook Primary School, Clydebank

My Friend

L ucky Liam gets sick
I ll Liam is very sick
A nxious Liam is worried
M agical Liam is magic.

Josh Innes (6)
Whitecrook Primary School, Clydebank

My First Acrostic - Southern Scotland Inspirations

My Friend

G enerous Georgia is afraid
E xploding Georgia
O riginal Georgia
R ainbow Georgia is so bright
G olden Georgia
I s a delightful friend
A lways wise.

Sophie Anderson (6)
Whitecrook Primary School, Clydebank

My Friend

D angerous David is
A dventurous, always
V anishes in thin air and he is
I nteresting, especially when he fights
D inosaurs.

Jay Scott (6)
Whitecrook Primary School, Clydebank

My First Acrostic - Southern Scotland Inspirations

My Friend

J ammy Josh is often fighting an
O stegosaurus
S hhh!
H ooray, he wins every time!

Liam Gallagher (6)
Whitecrook Primary School, Clydebank

My Friend

C hanelle is cool
H appy all the time
A nd can lift a crocodile
N obody can beat her, she's nice to everyone
E xtraordinary in every way
L ovely and kind
L ady Chanelle is
E xcellent!

Zoe Young (7)
Whitecrook Primary School, Clydebank

My First Acrostic - Southern Scotland Inspirations

Young Writers Information

We hope you have enjoyed reading this book - and that you will continue to enjoy it in the coming years.

If you like reading and writing poetry drop us a line, or give us a call, and we'll send you a free information pack.

Alternatively if you would like to order further copies of this book or any of our other titles, then please give us a call or log onto our website at www.youngwriters.co.uk.

Young Writers Information
Remus House
Coltsfoot Drive
Peterborough
PE2 9JX
(01733) 890066